Contents

Laying eggs

A butterfly is an **insect**.
An insect has six legs,
and **antennae**, or feelers,
on its head. In Spring,
a female butterfly lays
her eggs on leaves.

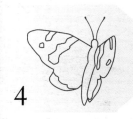

5

Inside the egg

The butterfly's eggs stick
to the leaves. Inside each
egg a **caterpillar** is growing.
It takes 10 days for the
caterpillar to grow.

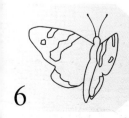

7

New caterpillar

A caterpillar hatches from the egg. The caterpillar eats leaves to help it grow. It makes a **leaf tent** to shelter in. It uses special silk to stick the leaves together.

9

Shedding skin

After a few days, the
caterpillar sheds its skin
so that it can grow bigger.
The caterpillar wraps itself
in leaves again while it
grows a new skin.

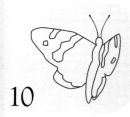

11

Fully grown

When a caterpillar is fully
grown, it gets ready to turn
itself into a butterfly.
It hangs from a leaf stem.

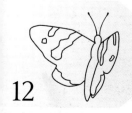   

Pupa

The caterpillar sheds its
skin again to form a **pupa**.
This takes a few hours.
The pupa is covered in a
cocoon. This keeps it safe.

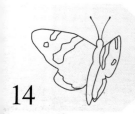   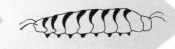

15

Changing

Inside the pupa, the caterpillar changes into a butterfly. After about three weeks the pupa splits open. A beautiful butterfly crawls out.

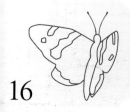   

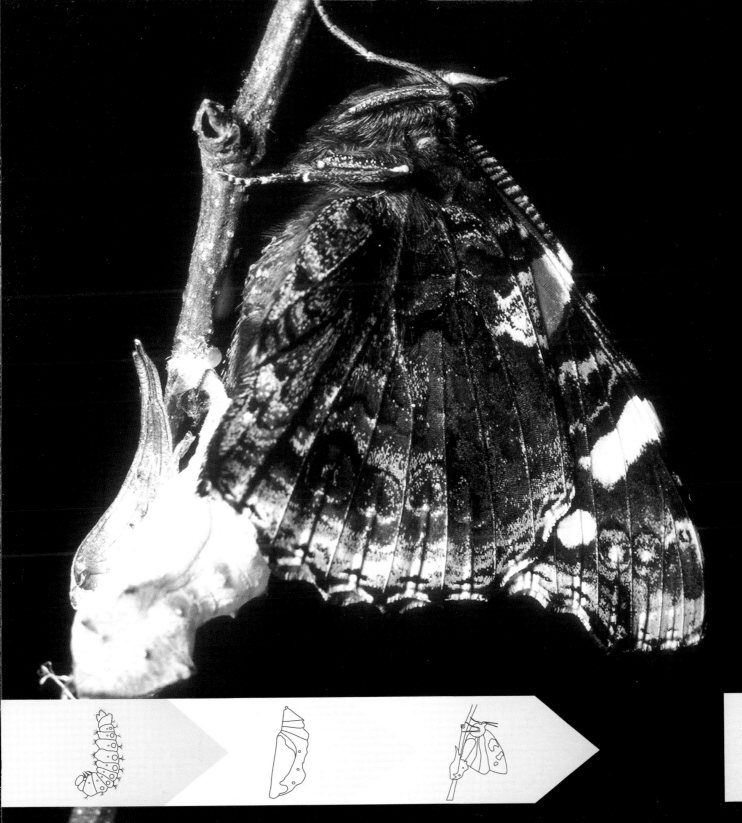

17

New butterfly

The new butterfly's wings are wrinkled. It climbs up the plant to shake out its wings. Then it flies away.

Flying away

In the Autumn some butterflies **migrate**. The butterflies fly to warmer countries. They come back in the Spring in time to lay their eggs on leaves.

Laying eggs	Inside an egg	New caterpillar	Shedding skin

Fully grown	Pupa	Changing	New butterfly

Butterfly facts

- The colour and shape of a butterfly's eggs are different for each type of butterfly.

- Some butterflies live for only three days, others can live for six months.

- Some butterflies can be as big as 30 cm wide.

- Some butterflies fly thousands of kilometres when they migrate.

- Butterflies taste with their feet. When they stand on food, they can taste it.

- A butterfly's tongue is like a drinking straw so that it can sip nectar from flowers. When it is not feeding, the tongue curls up out of the way.

- Butterflies' wings are covered with lots of tiny scales. This is what gives them their colour.

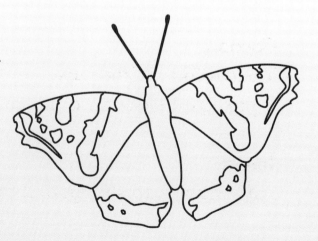

Butterfly words

Antennae
The feelers on the
head of an insect. They
are used for smelling.

Caterpillar
The stage in the life of a
butterfly between hatching from
an egg and forming a pupa.

Cocoon
The covering of the pupa.
It protects the caterpillar inside.

Insect
An animal with six legs and two
antennae. The body of an insect
is divided into three parts.

Leaf tent
Some caterpillars make a tent
from folded leaves to protect
them while they grow.

Migrate
To fly from one place to another
at regular times of the year.

Pupa
The stage in the life of a butterfly
between being a caterpillar and
becoming an adult butterfly.

Index